Fold out • Find out

The GIANT PANDA

Philip Steele
Illustrated by John Butler

About this book

The Giant Panda is almost like two books in one – a storybook to read and an information book to explore. Large, colourful illustrations and a simple narrative tell the story of the panda's life in the wild, while the text under the folds provides a mine of fascinating information.

If you are reading with a child, the underfold facts will give you the perfect opportunity to pause, answer questions and discuss what is happening in the story.

Children reading alone, will enjoy discovering the extra details under the folds, especially as the information they find there will enhance their understanding of the story.

After reading **The Giant Panda**, you may like to find out more about protecting pandas in the wild. If so, why not contact the local branch of an organization, such as the World Wide Fund for Nature, for more information.

It is dawn in the misty mountains of southwest China and a giant panda has just woken up from a deep restful sleep. She stretches and yawns, baring her pointed yellow teeth. Then she grabs the stem of some bamboo grass and starts to munch its spiky leaves.

Slowly, the panda shuffles out of the bamboo thicket. Eating bamboo makes her thirsty, so she sets off towards her favourite stream. Her great head sways from side to side as she plods along the valley bottom. Far above, thin white clouds are rolling back up the hillside. It is late spring and the rhododendron bushes are covered with beautiful pinky-red flowers.

China
pandaland

• Giant pandas **live in southwest China**, in Asia. The area in which they live is sometimes called 'pandaland'.

red panda

• There's **another kind of panda**, too. Some people call it the red panda after its red fur. Others call it the lesser panda because it's smaller than the giant panda. It's very shy.

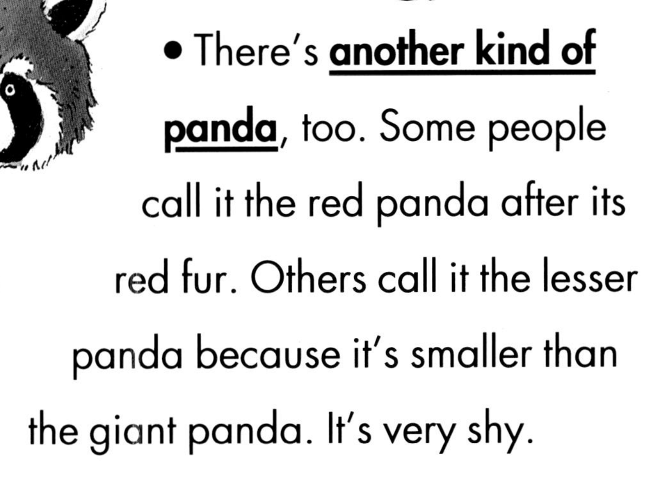

• The giant panda **isn't really a giant**. A full-grown male panda measures around 1.5 metres from its nose to its tail.

• A giant panda is heavy, though. A full-grown male panda can **weigh up to 150 kilograms**. That's the same as about SIX of you!

The panda stretches and yawns again. Then she lumbers off down a small moss-covered track. She's always hungry, so she stops to nibble a few crocuses on the way.

The panda ambles into the woods. She sniffs the air as she walks along a gloomy trail through the trees. Suddenly she stops. There's a strong smell of another animal nearby. Just ahead, the branches shake and rustle. Then, all at once, a startled face breaks through the bushes. It's a takin!

- Although pandas look cuddly, they have **strong jaws and sharp teeth**. Even fierce animals, such as wild dogs and panthers, wouldn't attack a full-grown panda.

- The **black-and-white fur** on a panda's face warns another animal: 'Stay away! I'm fierce!'

- Pandas **like to live alone**. They don't live in families or groups as many other animals do.

- Every panda has its **own private area** called its territory. One panda's territory may be right next to that of another panda. Even then, they usually don't make friends.

The panda snarls, though she knows the takin won't attack her. But the gentle takin is scared and it crashes off through the undergrowth in fright.

The panda reaches the stream and takes a long drink of cool clear water. There's a thick patch of bamboo growing nearby. She often likes to rest here, with her back against a mossy bank, while she chomps on the lush green bamboo shoots.

• Bamboo is a **giant grass** that grows all year round. There are many kinds of bamboo, but most pandas only eat four or five kinds.

• Pandas **spend a lot of time eating** – about 14 hours a day!

• Pandas have to eat a lot because **bamboo has little goodness in it**. Its sharp-edged leaves and tough stems would be about as tasty to us as a pencil sandwich!

• Pandas have an **extra 'thumb'** on each paw to grip the bamboo stems.

extra 'thumb'

Gripping
the bamboo
stems tightly
in her paw, she
munches the
leaves and
crunches the
tough stalks.

The weeks pass and spring turns into summer. One day, as the panda rests on the branch of a tree, it begins to rain. The rain runs in little rivers down the paths. It drums on the tree trunks and the leaves. And it trickles down the panda's nose! She doesn't mind a fine, cold drizzle but she hates the heavy rain.

• Pandas have a **thick coat of waterproof fur**. It keeps them dry in the rain and warm in the snow. The fur feels bristly when you stroke it.

• Pandas **like to swim**. They doggy-paddle along with their heads in the air. Their fur dries quickly after a dip.

• Pandas **like to roll in the dust**, too. This keeps their fur healthy and free from itchy mites.

Mites (tiny insects) hate the dust!

• A panda's **hairy feet and strong curved claws** help it to climb easily up tree trunks.

She climbs down and finds a dry, hollow tree trunk to shelter in. There, she has a nap and waits for the rain to ease.

Winter arrives, covering the mountains in a thick blanket of snow.

The panda has wandered towards the edge of her territory, looking for some tasty bamboo to eat. She pads down the hillside, leaving pawprints in the freshly fallen snow.

She stops... she can hear strange sounds ahead.

• The bamboo forests where pandas live have become **smaller and smaller**. People have cut down trees and farmers have built new villages.

• Pandas must be able to **move from one feeding place to another**. Sometimes all the bamboo in one area dies back and the pandas must find another kind of bamboo to eat until it grows again.

• **Villagers try to help pandas** but they often don't know what's best for them. Sometimes, villagers have 'rescued' a baby panda that they think is lost when really it isn't.

There are voices – coming closer! Then there's an excited shout! The panda is scared. She turns quickly and lumbers back into the safety of the forest.

When spring returns, fresh shoots of bamboo push their way through the warm soil and the streams become swollen with melted snow. One day the panda sees another black-and-white face peering through the undergrowth. It is a male panda. She grunts angrily and he moves away.

But the next day he's there again. She begins to feel more friendly towards him. They play together and soon they mate.

• Pandas are usually very quiet, but they **call to each other** when it's time to mate. They grunt, snort, growl and even bark.

• Pandas **leave smelly messages for each other**. They rub their bottoms against trees, leaving a sticky liquid which other pandas can 'read'.

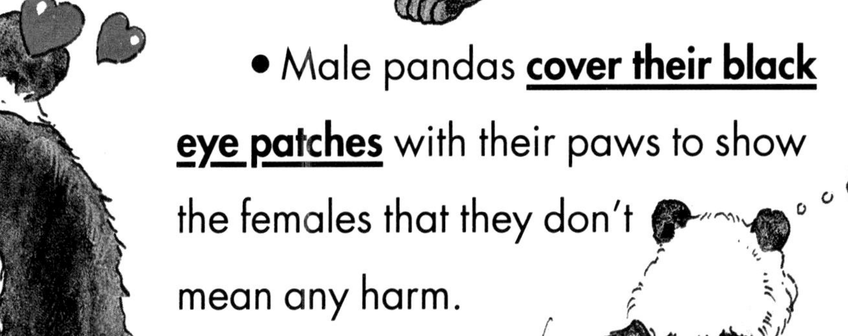

• Male pandas **cover their black eye patches** with their paws to show the females that they don't mean any harm.

• Zoos all over the world **try to help pandas to mate** and have babies. They introduce males and females but the pandas often ignore each other!

One bright day, six months later, the panda sniffs around a little cave she has found. It seems warm and dry. She pulls in twigs, bamboo stems and fir branches to make a bed. Then she settles down, blocking the entrance with her body to keep the cave snug and safe.

- Pandas **mostly have twins**, but only one cub usually lives. A panda may give birth to eight or nine cubs in her lifetime.

newborn
small and pink, cannot see, weighs just 100 grams

3 weeks
black-and-white markings show

10 weeks – eyes now open, mother may carry it gently in her mouth

- A **baby panda's skin** is dark where the black fur will grow and pale where the white fur will grow.

3 months
starts to crawl

6 months – starts to eat bamboo

1 year
can walk quite well, teeth have come through

- Pandas live until they are about **25 to 30 years old**.

Here, the panda has her baby cub. At first he is tiny, blind and helpless. But he soon grows, nourished by his mother's rich, warm milk.

The following winter is very cold. Fierce winds blow down the mountainside. Snow drifts into the bamboo thickets and icicles hang over the stream. Even so, the little panda cub grows big and strong. One day, as he plays in the snow near his mother, there's a flash of spotted fur in the bare branches above. It's a leopard!

- Although animals don't usually attack full-grown giant pandas, **cubs are sometimes killed** by foxes, wild dogs or leopards.

- In China, people sometimes tell the story of **how pandas got their black-and-white markings**. Long ago, they say, pandas' faces were completely white. One day, a little girl rescued a panda cub that was being attacked by a leopard. However, the fierce beast killed her instead. All the pandas in China cried when they heard the news. As they wiped their tears and held their heads in sorrow, their dark paws left black smudges around their eyes and ears.

Quickly, the cub's mother rears up, baring her pointed fangs. She snarls fiercely, and the leopard bounds away across the powdery snow.

A whole year passes and it is spring once more. The giant panda and her cub are searching for the tastiest, tenderest young bamboo shoots on the whole mountain. As they wander down the hillside, they hear voices. Down in the valley bottom, hidden in a clump of trees, there's an orange tent on a platform of logs.

• Scientists sometimes fit **radio collars** to the necks of wild pandas. The collars send out signals that tell the scientists where the pandas are. This helps scientists learn more about pandas – and the more they know, the more they can help.

• The number of pandas living in the wild has fallen to only 1,000. To help **save the panda**, the Chinese have opened special reserves to give pandas enough land to live on and enough to eat.

• The World Wide Fund for Nature helps to **protect animals in danger**. Its badge shows a giant panda.

The tent belongs to some Chinese scientists who have been studying giant pandas for several weeks. They are checking that the pandas are safe and have enough bamboo to eat.

The panda cub is one and a half now and big enough to look after himself. One morning, he leaves his mother as she is ambling along her usual path to the stream. He is ready to find his own territory, in another part of the bamboo forest.